EARLY PIONEERS

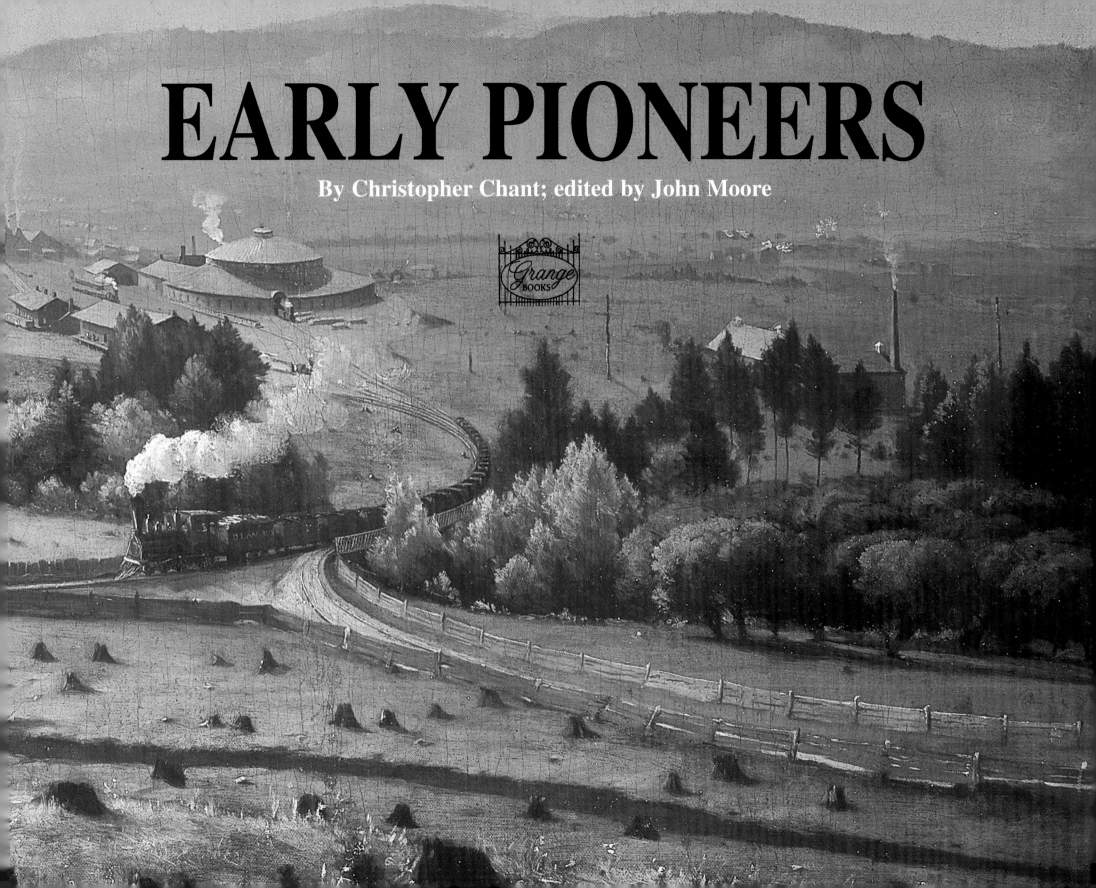

EARLY PIONEERS

By Christopher Chant; edited by John Moore

Grange
BOOKS

Published in 2002 by
Grange Books
An imprint of Grange Books Plc
The Grange
Kingsnorth Industrial Estate
Hoo, nr Rochester
Kent ME3 9ND
www.grangebooks.co.uk

ISBN 1 84013 356 2

Printed in Hong Kong

FAMOUS TRAINS

TITLE PAGE: *The Lackawanna Valley, by
George Inness.*

RIGHT: *The engine* Firefly *on a new
trestle built by the Union Construction
Corps on the Orange & Alexandria
Railroad during the American Civil War.*

PAGE 5: *Tin mine between Cambourne
and Redruth, Cornwall, England. From H.
Besley's* Views of Devonshire and
Cornwall, *Exeter, circa 1860.*

EARLY PIONEERS

The date 27 September 1825 is generally regarded as the beginning of the 'Railway Age', for on this day the word's first public steam line, the Stockton & Darlington Railway, opened for business. It should not be forgotten, however, that the day's run by George Stephenson's *Locomotion No. I* marked only one evolutionary and commercial stage in a process that had begun slowly many years earlier and was destined to proceed with increasing rapidity into the present.

This process may be deemed to have begun with the wooden tracks and wheeled trucks believed to have been used by German mining operators, possibly as early as the 12th century. Such a system, powered by men and/or draft animals, spread slowly to other mining areas of Europe, but became common in Britain only in the 17th century when systems of wooden tracks for wheeled trucks became increasingly common in the coal-mining regions of north-east England. Although workable, as indicated by the fact that it lasted for so long, the system was by no means fully practical, although a move in this direction came in the 18th century, when the wooden rails were replaced by cast iron rails that were considerably better lasting as well as

stronger than their wooden predecessors, and as such also paved the way for the advent of powered traction in the form of the steam locomotive, which became increasingly accepted in the first quarter of the 19th century.

The steam locomotive was a true child of the Industrial Revolution, and also helped to make this revolution the world-shattering force that it soon became. As is often the case with movements that rapidly become huge forces for change in the world, it is difficult to put a precise date on its beginning, but it is fair to say that by about 1760 in Britain the combination of scientific and technological development, the availability of raw materials such as iron and coal, and the entrepreneurial spirit was so stimulated that the process was inevitable. Thus the reign of King George III (1760–1820) may be taken as the beginning of the Industrial Revolution that turned the United Kingdom from a country that relied mainly on agriculture and trade for its livelihood into a country that based its living on the manufacture and export of goods.

In any such country the swift and economical delivery of raw materials to the factories, and the steady shipment of

George Stephenson (1781–1848), a British locomotive and railway pioneer, builder of the Rocket *and engineer for the Stockton & Darlington and Liverpool & Manchester Railways.*

finished goods to major cities and ports are both essential to economic success and continued growth. Canals certainly played their part in the movement of bulk freight such as coal and iron to the factories, but was too slow and roundabout for the outward movement of finished goods, which in any case needed to reach more destinations than could be served by the

geographically limited canal network, even when aided by horse-drawn wagons. Another factor of the Industrial Revolution that helped the invention and development of railways was the change in the pattern and distribution of the British population. Manufacturing industries had to be highly concentrated, leading to the rapid growth of the population of industrial cities: these new urban populations could not of course feed themselves, and their demand for food could only be met by the timely arrival of fresh produce from the surrounding countryside. And as the cities continued to grow as the Industrial Revolution gathered pace, the area from which food had to be shipped increased to the extent that only railways could supply the right quantities in the time before the food began to rot.

The single most important factor that allowed the development of a successful railway network in the United Kingdom was steam power, itself both a child of the early Industrial Revolution and parent of the later one. As suggested above, however, the 'railway concept' was much older than the Industrial Revolution. Certainly by the beginning of the 16th century, for example, German miners had found that it was easier to move their heavy loads of coal if their

BELOW: *An advertisement for the first passenger railway carriage called* The Experiment *to operate on the Stockton & Darlington Railway, whose main purpose was to transport coal.* The Experiment *was a crude version of an omnibus on wheels.*

RIGHT: *George III, 1738–1820 (reigned from 1760), shown in military uniform in a full-length portrait by William Beechey, (1775–1839).*

BELOW: *A railway in a mine. From Sebastian Munster's* Cosmographie, *1550. This is said to be the earliest picture of a railway.*

Stockton & Darlington Railway.
The Company's
◄ COACH ►
CALLED THE
EXPERIMENT,

Which commenced Travelling on MONDAY, the 10th of OCTOBER, 1825, will continue to run from *Darlington* to *Stockton*, and from *Stockton* to *Darlington* every Day, [Sunday's excepted] setting off from the DEPOT at each place, at the times specified as under, (viz.):----

ON MONDAY,

From Stockton at half-past 7 in the Morning, and will reach Darlington about half-past 9; the Coach will set off from the latter place on its return at 3 in the Afternoon, and reach Stockton about 5.

TUESDAY,

From Stockton at 3 in the Afternoon, and will reach Darlington about 5.

On the following Days, viz:----

WEDNESDAY, THURSDAY
& FRIDAY,

From Darlington at half-past 7 in the Morning, and will reach Stockton about half-past 9; the Coach will set off from the latter place on its return at 3 in the Afternoon, and reach Darlington about 5.

SATURDAY,

From Darlington at 1 in the Afternoon, and will reach Stockton about 3.

Passengers to pay 1s. each, and will be allowed a Package of not exceeding 14lb. all above that weight to pay at the rate of 2d. per Stone extra. Carriage of small Parcels 3d. each. The Company will not be accountable for Parcels of above £5 Value, unless paid for as such.

Mr RICHARD PICKERSGILL at his Office in Commercial Street, Darlington; and Mr TULLY at Stockton, will for the present receive any Parcels and Book Passengers.

cart wheels ran on smooth tracks. The solution was to lay parallel tracks of wooden planks over the rough ground and push the carts along them. The inevitable problem was how to prevent the carts from wandering off the tracks on their flat-rimmed wheels: the solution evolved by the middle of the 15th century in places such as Leberthal in Alsace was the railed cart, and by the middle of the 18th century this had been developed into a system of flanged metal wheels running on cast iron rails. This improved the overall capability of the system to the extent that horses could be used to haul the carts, which were soon developed into wagons with yet-heavier loads, on what became known as tramways or wagonways.

By the beginning of the 19th century steam was well established as the fixed power source driving the Industrial Revolution, most notably in the steam engines designed by James Watt in the 1780s, developments on originals by Thomas Newcomen: these were low-pressure beam engines, and were used principally to pump water out of mines. These early steam engines were not notably efficient, and were also very heavy. Even so, far-sighted inventors were already at work trying to develop a steam-powered form of transport. Two of the earliest pioneers were James Watt and William Murdoch, who sought to exploit the possibilities inherent in steam power for the creation of a mechanical road carriage.

GEO. STEPHENSON'S ROCKET, 1829.

Less far-sighted but eminently more practical was a Cornishman, Richard Trevithick, who appreciated that the best way to harness the power of current steam engines was in a locomotive for use on a wagonway. Starting work in the 1790s, Trevithick embarked on the design of high-pressure steam engines offering a considerably better power/weight ratio than their predecessors. It is to Trevithick that there falls the distinction of having built the world's first practical steam locomotive, which first ran at Coalbrookdale in Shropshire in 1803. Trevithick's next steam locomotive (page 13) was completed in the following year for use on the tramroad of the Pen-y-Darren ironworks in South Wales, and in trials proved itself able to haul wagons carrying 15 tons of iron. The third

TOP LEFT: *George Stephenson's* Rocket, *winner of the Rainhill Trials in 1829.*

TOP: The Pitman: *from George Walker's* The Costume of Yorkshire, *Leeds, 1814. Left of the picture is a steam locomotive built by Matthew Murray for John Blenkinsop which was used to haul coal from Middleton Colliery to Leeds.*

LEFT: *Barge viaduct over the Irwell on the Bridgewater Canal, England. Engineer: James Brindley.*

RIGHT: *Bottom of a pit shaft with a train of wagons waiting to be hoisted to the surface. Note the flanged wheels on the coal wagon. Picture first published in 1860.*

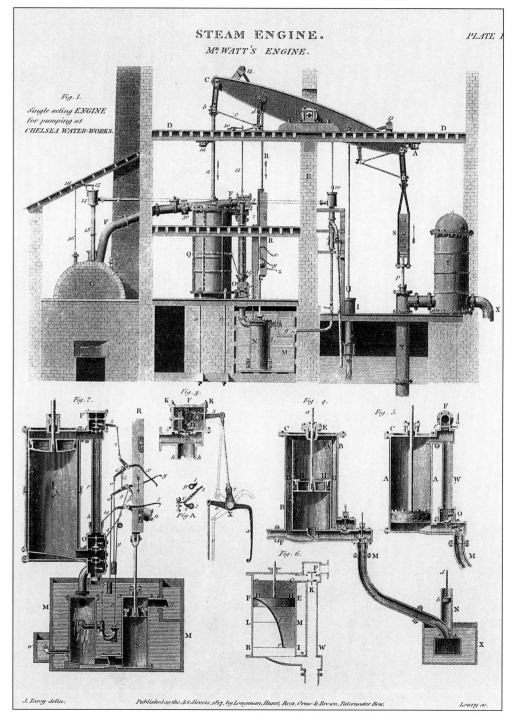

of Trevithick's engines was completed soon after this, and was the *Catch-Me-Who-Can*, a steam locomotive powered by a single vertical cylinder at the rear and which was demonstrated during 1808 near Euston in London (see page 12): behind a sturdy fence, the trials of this pioneering steam locomotive were undertaken on a circular track pulling a single carriage.

Trevithick's steam engines were of the type with a geared drive from a single front- or rear-located cylinder to smooth flanged wheels. The steam locomotives were in themselves moderately successful at the technical level, but their development was

TOP: *Wooden trucks on the wagonway at the head of the Derby Canal at Little Eaton. Coal from the Denby Colliery near Derby, England was loaded into these wagons and hauled by horses to the canal side, where is was loaded by crane, still in the wagon body, into canal boats for on-shipment. The tramway was built following an Act of Parliament of 1793 and operated until 1908.*

RIGHT: *Watt's steam engine, built for the Chelsea waterworks, London. From a print published in London in 1820.*

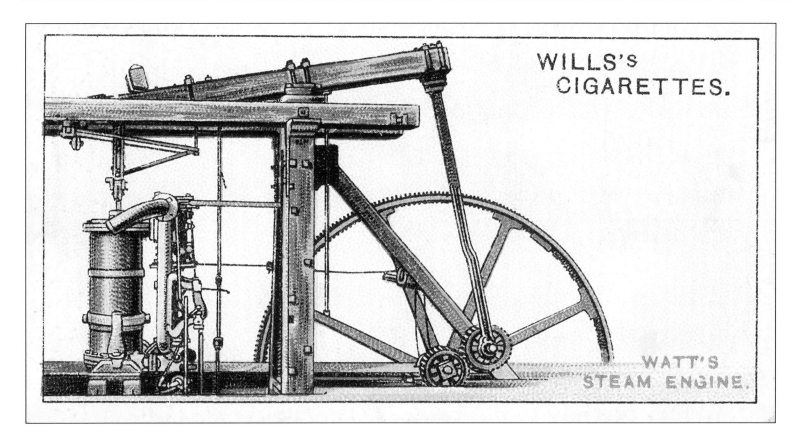

WILL'S CIGARETTES.

WATT'S STEAM ENGINE.

to a certain extent a dead end, for there was immense antipathy to the primitive wagonways by ironworkers and others who feared for the loss of their jobs if horses were replaced by steam locomotives. Moreover, the wagonways of the period were in any event insufficiently strong to carry the weight of the locomotive (derived from a stationary steam engine and therefore very heavy) without frequent breakages.

While the South Wales iron industry may have rejected the steam locomotive, the coal-mining industry of north-east England was more perceptive. In 1812 the Middleton Colliery Railway (established by Act of Parliament in 1758) started to use the world's first commercial steam locomotive, designed by Matthew Murray (page 13). This locomotive had two vertical cylinders and ran on strong cast iron rails, one of which had a rack section engaged by a matching rack on the locomotive's geared driving wheel to ensure maximum traction. By 1820 steam locomotives designed by Timothy Hackworth, George Stephenson and William Hedley were in service on the comparatively steep wagonways of the collieries at which these men were the chief engineers.

ABOVE: *A steam engine of James Watt's own design showing sun-and-planet gear converting up-and-down motion of beam to rotary motion for driving machinery. From a cigarette card published in 1915.*

ABOVE RIGHT: *Thomas Newcomen's schematic steam engine. A colour print published in London in the early 19th century. Newcomen lived from 1663–1729.*

RIGHT: *James Watt (1736–1819), Scottish engineer and inventor. From a chromolithograph published in London in 1824.*

LEFT and ABOVE: Catch-Me-Who-Can, a railway locomotive designed by Richard Trevithick in 1808. It was demonstrated on a circular track near to where Euston Station, London now stands.

OPPOSITE
TOP LEFT: Portrait of English engineer Richard Trevithick (1771–1833) after the 1816 portrait by John Linnell. Trevithick specialized in the design of high-pressure road and railway locomotives.

TOP RIGHT: Trevithick's high-pressure tram engine for Pen-y-Darren ironworks, South Wales (1804).

BELOW: Steam locomotive built by Matthew Murray for John Blenkinsop and used to haul coals from Middleton Colliery to Leeds, beginning in August 1912.

in Northumberland ran on flanged wheels with the driving wheels powered by two vertical cylinders powering a chain drive between the axles.

All of these pioneering efforts were undertaken on private 'railways' designed solely for the movement of coal and some of the collieries' heavy equipment. Considerable design, manufacturing and operating experience had been gained, however, and this proved invaluable when the world's first public steam railway was planned. The spur for this development was the need of local businessmen to move coal as well as goods between the mines in the south of County Durham and the port of Stockton on the River Tees. The local consortium employed the self-taught Stephenson, a young colliery engineer from Northumberland, as the chief engineer of the Stockton & Darlington Railway. Stephenson designed and supervised the construction of the track, and also designed and built the pioneering steam locomotive *Locomotion No. I*, which as noted above initiated the 'Railway Age' in September 1825 by hauling a load of 68 tons along the 21-mile (34-km) track from Shildon to Stockton. There was enormous enthusiasm for the overall concept, but the fact that people did not altogether trust the concept of steam locomotion is demonstrated in its first eight years of operation in that the Stockton & Darlington Railway moved only coal and goods under steam power, people being transported in horse-drawn carriages.

Even so, George Stephenson must be regarded as the 'father of the railway'.

Hedley's *Puffing Billy* (page 14), introduced in 1813, was a notable advance over its predecessors as it was driven by a single crank on one side. As originally completed, the *Puffing Billy* had a 0-4-0 configuration, but was then revised to a 0-8-0 layout in an effort to better cope with the poor track on which it ran, but then reverted to the original configuration. Hedley's next steam locomotive was the *Wylam Dilly*. Stephenson's 0-4-0 steam locomotive of 1815 for the Killingworth Colliery Railway

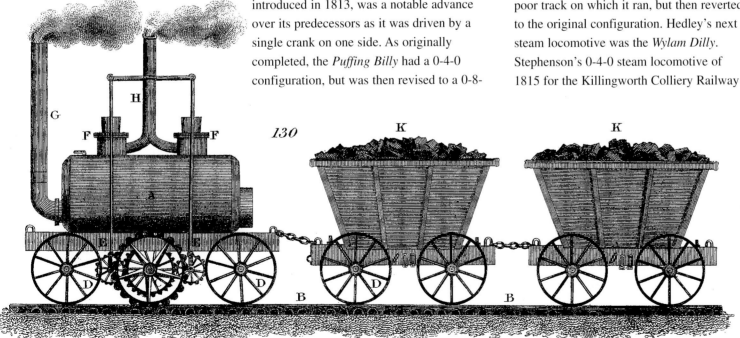

OPPOSITE

TOP LEFT: William Hedley's Puffing Billy *(1813). From Amédée Guillemin's* The Applications of Physical Force, *London, 1877.*

TOP RIGHT: The Baltimore & Ohio Tom Thumb *locomotive, with additional horse power.*

BELOW LEFT: An early 1850s Baltimore & Ohio train with stagecoach and covered wagon.

BELOW RIGHT: The Experiment, the first passenger coach built by George Stephenson for the Stockton & Darlington Railway in 1825.

Despite the technical success of *Locomotion No. I*, the Stockton & Darlington Railway did not become the world's first steam-worked 'inter-city' passenger line for, after the inaugural run, passenger services reverted to horse power.

Thus it was not until the inauguration of the Liverpool & Manchester Railway in the course of September 1830 that the world's first genuine passenger-carrying railway came into existence. Designed by Stephenson, the Liverpool & Manchester Railway had to overcome considerable engineering difficulties, including that of crossing Chat Moss Bog, and made use of new and more reliable steam locomotives, such as the *Rocket* designed by Robert

Stephenson, George Stephenson's even more talented son.

This was only the beginning of the story, though, and in the mainland of the European continent the introduction of steam railways followed not long after those in the U.K. The first French railway, extending between St.-Étienne and Andrézieux, started operation with horse power in October 1828. Developments in France were comparatively slow at this

BELOW LEFT: Blenkinsop's cog railway, 1811. This ran from Middleton to Leeds, a distance of 3½ miles (5.6km), and was used to haul coals.

BELOW: George Stephenson's engine Locomotion. *From Louis Figuier's* Les Nouvelles Conquêtes de la Science, *Paris circa 1890.*

HOW TO INSURE AGAINST RAILWAY ACCIDENTS.

TIE A COUPLE OF DIRECTORS À LA MAZEPPA TO EVERY ENGINE THAT STARTS WITH A TRAIN.

NAVVY IN HEAVY MARCHING ORDER.

STEPHENSON TEACHING THE NAVVIES.

time, however, and by a time as late as 1850 there were a mere 1,927 miles (3100 km) of railway in that country when compared to the British figure of more than 6,600 miles (10620km) in a geographically smaller country. This was an odd time for the development of modern technology in France, and lack of adequate indigenous capabilities (in terms of engineering skills, financial resources and even labourers) meant that the U.K. played a major role in the development of the French railway network in the form of financiers to make the development possible, civil engineers to lay out and build the tracks (often with the

aid of 'navvies' imported from the U.K.), and mechanical engineers to design and manufacture the required steam locomotives and rolling stock.

It was not long after the establishment of the first British railways that the concept crossed the Atlantic Ocean to the United States of America. This, the first U.S. railroad to launch services was the Baltimore & Ohio Railroad that began, with horse-drawn carriages, in the course of April 1827. The first steam locomotives did not arrive in the U.S.A. until 1829 when the distinction of being the first steam locomotive to run on an American railroad,

in this instance the Delaware & Hudson Railroad, was secured by the *Stourbridge Lion* (page 20), one of four locomotives bought in the U.K. and shipped across the Atlantic. The locomotive was too heavy for the rails, however, for these rails were of iron-plated wooden construction, and the Delaware & Hudson had therefore to return to horse power for several more years.

It was the Baltimore & Ohio that succeeded, on 25 August 1830, in making the first public run of the first American-built steam locomotive, named the *Tom Thumb*. Within a year of this important

date, U.S. railroads were becoming increasing well established with steam power, the next two entrants onto this scene being the Camden & Amboy and the Mohawk & Hudson Railroads.

The technical and commercial success of the early railways and railroads spawned a 'vicious circle' in reverse: success spurred the start of more companies, and the continued spread of railway and railroad availability in Europe and the eastern side of the U.S.A. encouraged the growth in passenger and freight traffic, which in turn laid the groundwork for the further expansion of the railway and railroad

networks and the launching of new companies.

This rapidly overcame the often high levels of suspicion and indeed fear with which steam locomotives had initially been greeted. By the early 1840s, railways and railroads were so popular with the public in general that investors were more than happy to begin pouring capital into existing and also new companies. The result was a huge boom in the financial importance of railways and railroads in a process that was inflated by the general perception that travel behind a steam locomotive was extremely safe and the very epitome of 'modern' peace and prosperity.

This 'railway boom' inevitably led to

failures. Some plans for new railways were realistic, but many others were not, and the period was characterized by the floating of huge numbers of schemes in what became known as 'railway mania'. (*The Times* suggested in 1845 that more than 600 new lines had already been proposed for construction in the U.K., with another 600 likely to be proposed and indeed accepted in the near future.) Lack of financial prudence and the possibility of apparently limitless profits to be made from railway construction and operations persuaded large numbers of investors, small as well as large, to risk their entire capital in railway shares. As is so often the case, however, the 'boom' was followed by a 'bust', in this instance sparked in 1847 when the Bank of England raised its interest rate and investors

panicked. Typical of those who eventually lost out was George Hudson (1800–1871), a businessman from York who after receiving a legacy decided to invest in railways and developed the capability of driving down the shares of rival companies so that he could then buy them cheaply and so gain control. Hudson became a member of parliament and by 1846, as the British 'railway king', directly controlled 20 per cent of the British railway system as well as exercising a strong influence over another 30 per cent before his fall as a result of the 'bursting' of the railway bubble and the revelation that he had used illegal methods.

Except in France, the railways of Europe expanded dramatically in extent during a short period, and thus mirrored the corresponding British railway mania. The

first steam railway in Bavaria, still an independent kingdom in southern Germany in this period before the unification of 1871, saw the start on 7 December 1835 of its first steam railway, named the Ludwigsbahn in honour of King Ludwig and which extended between Fürth and Nuremburg. This operation used rails and rolling stock manufactured in Germany, but its first steam locomotive was *Der Adler* (The Eagle), an example of the 'Patentee' design built by Robert Stephenson & Company. Other earlier railways completed in Germany included the Saxon State Railway inaugurated in 1837, with a service between Dresden and Leipzig, and a Prussian operation launched in the following year with a line linking Berlin and Potsdam.

European enthusiasm for the railway

can be gauged from the fact that initial lines came into existence in Belgium during 1835, in Austria during 1837, the Netherlands during 1839 and in Switzerland during 1844. Progress in Italy was slower, for this region was akin to Germany in that period, being a conglomerate of many small and notionally independent states. Thus the first Italian railway appeared only in October 1839 as a line linking Naples and Portici.

The introduction of railways farther from the U.K. took place slightly later, and the development of railways in these areas was generally slower than in the U.K., Western Europe, the U.S.A. and, to a more limited extent, Canada. In these industrially less advanced regions there was no railway mania. In the Scandinavian area, the first

OPPOSITE

LEFT: *The* DeWitt Clinton, *built for the Mohawk & Hudson Railroad by the West Point Foundry, which made the 17-mile (27-km) trip from Albany to Schenectady in less than an hour.*

RIGHT: *The David & Gartner locomotive* Grasshopper *of the Baltimore & Ohio Railroad was built in the 1830s.*

THIS PAGE RIGHT: *The locomotive* Atlantic *with a pair of Imlay coaches, built for the Baltimore & Ohio Railroad in 1832.*

BELOW RIGHT: *Construction crew at work on the Northern Pacific Railroad.*

country to introduce a railway was Denmark, where in 1844 the Baltic Line was created to link Altona with Kiel in 1844. As well as having a relative lack of industrial capability, the development of railways in Scandinavia was also made difficult by the harsher climatic and geographical features of the area, and as a result the first Norwegian and Swedish railways did not start business until 1854 and 1856 respectively.

In Russia, the country's first railway was the St. Petersburg and Pavlovsk, which began a mainly horse-drawn service between Tsarskoye Selo and Pavlovsk, using a track gauge of 6ft 0in (1.83m), although the launch of work on the line between Moscow and St. Petersburg in 1851 saw the switch to the 5-ft (1.52-m) gauge still used in the countries of the former Russian Empire, later to become the Soviet Union and which is now the Commonwealth of Independent States.

Although the advent of the railway had been initially viewed with modest suspicion that later turned to great enthusiasm, there were some who foresaw major catastrophe, fearing that those of nervous disposition (as well as children and animals) would be terrified and that the large-scale ruination of the land was imminent as a result of steam and smoke emissions. Experience soon revealed these fears to be without foundation, and railways soon became accepted in Europe and North America as increasingly 'natural' elements of the landscape in an ever more industrialized age. Simple habituation with the railway

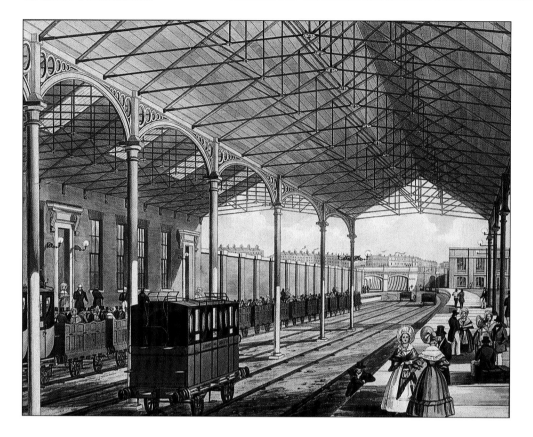

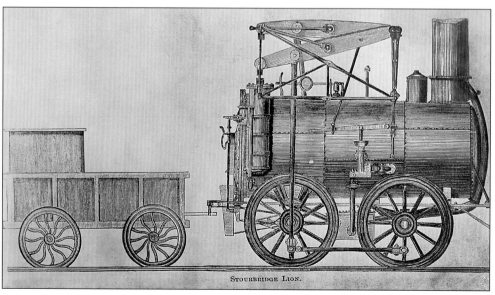

STOURBRIDGE LION.

WILLS's CIGARETTES

⑦

1ST LOCOMOTIVE IN THE U.S.A.

ABOVE: *Early U.S. engineers surveying in Cheat River Valley for the Baltimore & Ohio Railroad in the late 1840s.*

RIGHT: *Laying the first stone of the Baltimore & Ohio Railroad on 4 July 1828.*

OPPOSITE
ABOVE LEFT: *A view of Euston Station, London in 1837.*

ABOVE RIGHT: *The opening of the first railway in Canada between La Prairie and St. Johns on 21 July 1836.*

BELOW LEFT and RIGHT: *Two depictions of the* Stourbridge Lion. *It was built in England under the direction of Horatio Allen and was the first locomotive to be used in America, where it was bought to work the Delaware & Hudson Railroad in 1829.*

was one of the reasons for its rapid acceptance, but another was the enormously improved levels of comfort and speed that railway services were able to provide. Opened for service in 1841, for instance, the Great Western Railway offered a journey time between London and Bristol of a mere five hours in comparison to at least 24 and often 48 hours required by the horse-drawn coach services on a road that was very poor despite the fact that it linked two of England's major cities.

Travel by rail was, in its early days, very much something of an adventure, and it was only from 1890 that the standard of overall comfort improved dramatically. In the early days of rail travel, passengers travelling on a first-class ticket had good seats in compartments with glass windows, but there was neither heating nor any corridor linking the various compartments or carriages. Passengers in second-class accommodation had a reduced level of comfort in carriages that were roofed, like those of the first-class passengers, but there was no glass in the windows. Worst off were those travelling third-class in open carriages without roofs, where they were exposed to smoke and sparks pouring from the locomotive's stack.

The profit made from third-class passengers was so small that many companies provided no such accommodation, or ran trains for third-class passengers at wholly inconvenient times and slow speeds. In 1844, however, a third-class passenger froze to death in an open carriage of the Great Western Railway near

Reading in Berkshire, and as a result of the ensuing public outcry, an Act of Parliament was passed ordaining that each railway line should provide at least one covered carriage per day for third-class passengers, who were to be charged no more than 1 penny per mile.

Early trains also lacked the facilities to offer passengers refreshment, and it was not until the later part of the 19th century that restaurant cars became common. Up to that time, passengers were wholly reliant on food they provided for themselves, or had to take what could be bought at stations,

which varied enormously in quality and price.

Another factor that helped rail travel to acquire a measure of common acceptance, especially among the middle classes, was the royal approval of the new transport system provided by Queen Victoria's 1842 journey from Slough, near Windsor in Berkshire, to Paddington in west London. The availability of rail travel now started to change the nature of British society with increasing speed from this time forward, and though most rail travel was the province of the affluent, who could afford first- and second-class accommodation, the poor were still able to travel by rail in the specially arranged excursions, generally between cities and nearby rural beauty spots or coastal resorts that became increasingly popular as the rail network expanded.

On the other side of the Atlantic, the period between the arrival of rail travel and the outbreak of the Civil War in 1861 was marked by a rail mania not unlike that which had swept the U.K. Increasing numbers of railroad companies were established in the states along America's eastern seaboard, most of these producing lines which stretched parallel to the coast; but increasingly, these north/south lines were connected by lateral east/west ones that were swiftly extended westward to the more heavily populated states of the hinterland and also to points on the great rivers and lakes (typically the Mississippi, Missouri and Ohio rivers and Lake Erie) that were the jumping-off points for the increasing numbers of people heading west in wagons in search of new land. Among the 'classic' lines of this period were those connecting Baltimore in Maryland with St. Louis in Missouri, Richmond in Virginia to Memphis in Tennessee, and New York to Lake Erie.

The rapidly developing railroad network therefore allowed the possibility for settlers to move west in larger numbers and begin the process of opening up new territories that the U.S. Government rightly judged to be the practical way of extending the size of the U.S.A. It was within the

ABOVE: *Images of the Baltimore & Ohio Railroad locomotives showing early and late steam examples.*

ABOVE RIGHT: *Train and coaches, the first to come from Baltimore to York in 1838.*

RIGHT: *Nickel's* Atmospheric *Railway carriage of 1845.*

OPPOSITE
ABOVE and BELOW: *Prosser's Wood Guide-Wheel Railway with engine, tender and carriage, operating on Wimbledon Common, London in 1845.*

In 1862, therefore, Congress passed the Pacific Railroad Bill into law, although it was not until the end of the Civil War that work was initiated by two companies. In the east was the Union Pacific Railroad, and in the west the Central Pacific Railroad. The two organizations were given enormous incentives to complete the railroad link as quickly as possible, which included a grant of land to a distance of 10 miles (16km) in alternating strips on each side of the track they laid, and loans of up to $48,000 per mile to help finance construction. There was an inadequate pool of cheap labour for the task within the U.S.A. and as a result large numbers of labourers were shipped in from China. Even so, the railroad link was an enormous and daunting task that was at times hampered by extremes of climate and geography as the two halves of the railroad forged from west and east.

Even so, the transcontinental railroad link across the United States was completed in just four years (rather than the 10 years that had originally been

context of this notion of 'manifest destiny' (a U.S.A. spanning the continent from the Atlantic to the Pacific oceans) that the idea of creating a transcontinental railroad line was first introduced during the Civil War (1861–1865). California, northward to Oregon and Washington, was already part of the United States, but President Abraham Lincoln had realized that if these areas were not to become isolated by the plains and deserts to the east of the Rocky Mountains, a transcontinental railroad link was essential.

ABOVE: *The Conestogo covered wagon and the classic American 4-4-0 locomotive did more than any other types of transport to open up the West.*

LEFT: *Opening of the Leipzig–Althen line in Germany in 1837.*

Roseby's Rock —
On Christmas Eve, 1852, the
Baltimore and Ohio Linked
Baltimore with the Ohio River,
thus fulfilling the Original Pur-
pose of Its Founders

ABOVE: *A Currier & Ives lithograph of the Niagara Suspension Bridge between the U.S.A. and Canada, 1856.*

ABOVE RIGHT: *An American railroad scene: clearing the snow from the track.*

LEFT: *Navvies at work at Roseby's Rock on the Baltimore & Ohio Railroad, December 1852.*

estimated) and tracks from west and east met on 10 May 1869 at Promontory Point in Utah to create a railroad line some 1,780 miles (2865km) long. A valuable off-spin was the establishment of a transcontinental telegraph service which was developed in parallel to the railroad.

Although the transcontinental railroad link was vitally important for the continued development of America into a single nation in the aftermath of the Civil War, it was by no means the only development of its type. In order to open up additional parts of the western United States, other railroad companies also received comparable land grant aid. The Chicago & North Western, the Burlington, and the Rock Island Railroad companies were only some of the

organizations that received significant incentives to provide profit as they forced the expansion of their lines. By 1890, other railroads had been completed to expand the connection across the U.S.A. These were the Southern Pacific, the Northern Pacific and the Atchison, Topeka & Santa Fe Railroads.

The extraordinary extent and pace of railroad expansion is illustrated most tellingly by a simple statistic: in 1845 there had been slightly more than 9,000 miles (14485km) of railroad line, but by 1890 this had increased to a figure of more than 163,500 miles (263120km).

The development of railroads in Central and South America was a lengthy and complicated matter. The railroad in Mexico

LEFT: *A restored* DeWitt Clinton *locomotive of the Albany & Hudson Railroad in 1831, connecting Albany and Schenectady .*

BELOW LEFT: *The locomotive* Chesapeake, *the first practical 4-6-0 engine built by Septimus Norris in 1847.*

OPPOSITE
LEFT: *One of Andrew Onderdonk's construction crews laying railway tracks in the Lower Fraser Valley, British Columbia.*

RIGHT: *The Toggenburg train arriving at Lichtensteig station in 1870, in north-eastern Switzerland.*

BELOW: *A ticket of 1835 for the Belgian railway.*

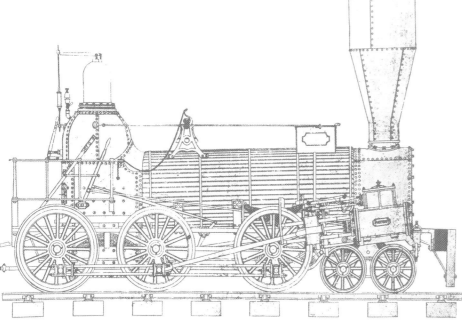

is somewhat atypical, for this substantial network was created between 1880 and 1900, largely with U.S. engineering skills and financing. The Panama Railroad, opened in 1855 long before the excavation of the Panama Canal that made its largely redundant from 1905, was constructed for the important task of moving passengers and, more importantly, freight across this narrowest point of the Central American isthmus, thereby allowing ships to avoid making the long and dangerous passage around Cape Horn and thus providing greater ease of travel, especially for journeys between the U.S.A.'s eastern coast and the Far East.

The development of railroads in South

America began somewhat later than in the U.S.A., and was again made possible largely by external finance, although in this instance the capital was provided by European nations rather than the U.S.A. The task of creating an effective railroad network over so vast an area was difficult enough in itself, but was also exacerbated by extremes of climate and geography as well as by frequent instability in the realms of national and international politics.

The development of railroad networks in Africa generally reflected the nature of the various regions and the ambitions of their colonial masters, most notably Belgium, France, Germany and the U.K. In general, each colony was served by a

line extending through British territory to link Cape Town in South Africa with Cairo (or more importantly Alexandria) in Egypt and thus provide a magnificent north-south route linking most of the British possessions in South, Central and North Africa. This far-sighted, even visionary scheme was terminated by the outbreak of World War I (1914–1918) after which no further progress was made and the line unfortunately came to an end in Rhodesia (now Zimbabwe).

Rhodes played an important part in the race between British and Dutch commercial interests to create a railroad link between South African ports and the gold-mining region of the Witwatersrand. In the event, Rhodes's driving force was largely responsible for the success of the British

slowly expanding network of services linking the main port or ports with the hinterland that might produce export cargoes and need the input of European equipment; but the single most ambitious scheme was Cecil Rhodes's 'Cape to Cairo'

Cape Government Railway in reaching Johannesburg in September 1892.

The first stage in the development of the world's initial flush of railroad building can be said to have ended in March 1899 when the Great Central Railway, which was the final large-scale railway programme of the age of Queen Victoria, began operation and in the process ended a period of just under three-quarters of a century of almost frantic railway development since the opening of the Stockton & Darlington Railway in 1825. This period had witnessed

revenues), and a measure of internal consolidation as a number of less successful companies were taken over or merged with more successful ones, resulting in the loss of once-celebrated names such as the Liverpool & Manchester and the London & Birmingham. In overall terms, the network of railway lines in the U.K. had reached its definitive goal that was only marginally altered by a small number of later additions.

Just as significantly, the cost of a journey had been vastly reduced in real terms, and rail was now very much the

developments that had made the train considerably faster as well as safer and also more comfortable. By about 1850, the standard design for a steam locomotive was virtually standardized as a 2-2-2 layout, but 50 years later the 4-4-0 layout was mostly standard on the longer British services. Hand-in-hand with improvements in the technology of train movement proper were important advances in other aspects of railway operation, including features such as the Westinghouse braking system, more effective signalling, and the interlinking of

OPPOSITE
LEFT ABOVE and BELOW: Pope Pius IX and the papal train in Italy in the 1860s.

RIGHT ABOVE: Locomotive pulling a train towards the Mont Cenis Tunnel which linked France with Italy. This was the first of the great alpine tunnels to be completed. From The Illustrated London News, *1869.*

RIGHT BELOW: The station at Campobasso, Italy, 1883.

LEFT: An early mixed passenger-freight train on the Belgian State Railway.

enormous developments in bringing a measure of sophistication to the railroad, both in steam locomotive technology and such ancillary services as signalling, the construction of a vast rail network linking virtually every populated region of the U.K. (often by two different companies, each with its own station, as a result of rivalry between companies to secure the maximum possible numbers of passengers and their

standard means of travel for all classes of society in the absence of rivals such as internal combustion-engined road vehicles although, for any with eyes to see, the writing was on the wall as the first primitive cars made an appearance.

Part of the pre-eminence of the train, hauled by a steam locomotive, stemmed from the absence of any realistic rival, but also from the rapid pace of technical

signals and points, which had done wonders to improve public confidence in the train, not only as a means of getting from one place to another in comfort at a moderately high speed, but also for travelling from one place to another in safety without the possibility of collision or failure to stop when required.

Also worthy of note in this area of British railway development was the

LEFT: An early track inspection car and crew, circa 1890.

OPPOSITE
LEFT: The highly spectacular steel Lethbridge Viaduct under construction, Alberta, Canada.

RIGHT: S.S. Slocan *at the wharf at Rosebery, British Columbia with the Canadian Pacific passenger train coming in from Nakusp 30 miles (48km) to the north. The train discharged passengers at Rosebery destined for points south on Slocan Lake, the remaining passengers going east to Sandon or Kaslo on Lake Kootenay.*

solution of the 'Gauge Question', which made standard a single track gauge for British railway lines and thereby made it eventually possible for any combination of steam locomotive and rolling stock to travel virtually the whole extent of the British network. After considerable deliberation and argument, in 1850 a royal commission ruled that the British national track gauge should be 4ft 8½in (1.432m) rather than the figure of 7ft 0in (2.436m) that had been adopted by the Great Western Railway at the instigation of the great engineer Isambard Kingdom Brunel. The Great Western Railway began to modify its track network in the early part of the 1870s, but completed the task only in 1892 with the conversion of the final stretch in the line extending between Paddington in London and Penzance in Cornwall.

This development of the railway networks, and the consolidation of the companies operating trains over them, was mirrored in Europe over much the same period, and at much the same time the separate railway networks of each country were gradually linked together to create a greater system of lines covering most of industrialized Europe and many lesser regions. Germany, however, made the slowest progress in this direction where efforts at rationalization were effectively stymied by the fact that until 1871, and the creation of a unified Germany after the

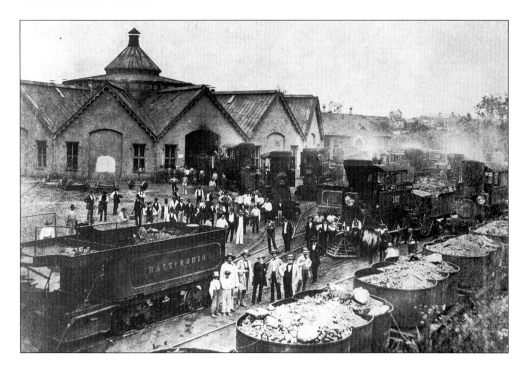

Franco-Prussian War of that year, Germany was a hotchpotch of large and smaller states, all of which guarded their 'individualities' with enormous zeal.

One of the main beneficiaries of this creation of a pan-European railway network was the Compagnie des Wagons-Lits established by Georges Nagelmackers, a Belgian, to provide services of the highest quality for the rich in the form of extremely comfortable accommodation (including sleeper berths for the night sections of these long-distance routes), excellent facilities and the best of food and wine. The most celebrated of the Wagons-Lits' services was the *Orient Express* from Paris in France to Constantinople (now Istanbul) in Turkey, but other notable services were the *Calais–Nice–Rome Express* and the *Sud*

RIGHT: *Poster advertising train tickets at Hornellsville for the Erie Railway.*

OPPOSITE
TOP LEFT: *Baltimore & Ohio Railroad 'Camelbacks' at Martinsburg, Virginia with, in the foreground, a coal train bound for Baltimore in 1858.*

TOP RIGHT: *The original Stoney Creek Bridge, British Columbia.*

BELOW: *The Bridge at Canyon Diablo in Arizona on the Atchison, Topeka & Santa Fe Railroad.*

Express linking Paris with the Portuguese capital of Lisbon via Madrid.

The railway network grew only slowly in Russia, where a mere 108 miles (174km) in 1850 was extended in the following 20 years to just 5,000 miles (8050km). During the next 30 years, however, there was a major surge in Russian railway-building with the result that by the turn of the century its network totalled more than 27,000 miles (43450km), including the justly celebrated

Trans-Siberian Railway connecting Moscow in western Russia with Vladivostok on the Pacific Ocean and by extension Port Arthur. Work on the Trans-Siberian Railway began in 1891 and was completed just under 10 years later after prodigious efforts under extraordinarily difficult conditions.

Farther to the east, Japan inaugurated its first railway in 1872. This was relatively late in comparison with many other countries as a result of the country's

essential medievalism in the period leading up to the Meiji restoration and the decision to turn Japan into a modern industrial nation; but Japan then made rapid strides and by 1890 possessed some 1,500 miles (2400km) or more of track.

By 1900, therefore, the impact of the railway and railroad as a force for economic and social change was fully evident, not least for its part in the creation and exploitation of the mass transportation market. Scrutiny of revenues

reveals that it was the transport of goods that yielded the greater part of the profits even though this was the more unglamorous aspect of the business, the imagination of the public having been caught more fully by passenger operations in general, and express passenger services in particular. The glamour attached to express passenger services should not be decried, moreover, for it was this aspect of the rail business, with its higher passenger revenues, that introduced restaurant

carriages as well as ones for passengers that were smoother-running and therefore more comfortable, and also pioneered innovatory features such as corridors linking compartments, toilet facilities and effective heating. The increasing levels of comfort evident from 1890 in longer-distance express services marked a major change in the concept of passenger travel, and the features soon became so standardized that they began to be extended further down the ladder, becoming available to ordinary passengers travelling shorter distances.

The need to cater for the creature comforts of the larger numbers of passengers paying lower fares was also spurred by the competition between rail companies, especially when two of these

were serving the same area and the competition between them was at its most direct. Another facet of this competition was speed of service, for it soon came to be appreciated that, in general, passengers preferred the faster service even if this meant travelling in slightly less comfortable surroundings.

OPPOSITE

TOP: *Baltimore & Ohio 4-4-0 Locomotive No. 232, built by William Mason at Taunton, Massachusetts in 1875 and seen here along the Potomac river near Cumberland, Maryland.*

BELOW LEFT: *The four-tiered 780-ft (238-m) long trestle built by Union engineers at Whiteside, Tennessee. 1864.*

BELOW RIGHT: *A train ticket of 1858 for the Canadian Grand Trunk Railway from Toronto to Grafton.*

THIS PAGE TOP: *Canadian Pacific Railway construction workers.*

BELOW LEFT: *1868. Construction work on cut No.1 west of the Narrows, Weber Canyon. The Narrows are situated 4 miles (6km) west of Echo and 995 miles (1600km) west of Omaha and presented some of the most difficult grading in the building of the Union Pacific Railroad. Successive shelves were hacked into the rock, then pickaxed and blasted down to grade. Rough, temporary tracks were laid to haul away rubble, while two-wheeled mule carts and wheelbarrows did the job on higher levels.*

FAR RIGHT: *Section gangs, like this Chicago, Burlington & Quincy crew, rode the rails on handcars to replace rotted ties, tamp loose spikes and tighten bolts. As a memento of their shared sense of responsibility, they struck this pose in the 1870s, their foreman's solemn little daughter in a place of honour.*

As noted above, in the U.K. many towns (many of them comparatively small) had at least two railways serving them. For instance, the Great Western Railway and the London & North Western Railway companies each operated on the route linking London and Birmingham and, in the period around the turn of the century, there was intense rivalry between the two to secure the lion's share of the market by providing a two-hour service between the British capital and its main manufacturing centre in the Midlands.

The distances covered by many railroad companies in the U.S.A. were generally considerably greater than their counterparts in the U.K., due to the U.S.A.'s generally lower population density and far larger geographical extent. This in no way lessened the rivalry between operators, however, for the same factor of directly competing services was often present. For instance, the route linking New York and Chicago in Illinois, both of them major centres of population, financial services and industry, pitted the New York Central Railroad and the Pennsylvania Railroad companies against one another and by 1902 the Pennsylvania Railroad had trimmed the time of its *Pennsylvania Special* express service to 20 hours.

Railways and railroads also played a not inconsiderable part in creating the nature and extent of the modern cities and conurbations through the inauguration of train services for commuters. This is inevitably a chicken-and-egg situation in which the question of which came first

OPPOSITE: The arrival of the first train into Vancouver, British Columbia on 23 May 1887.

RIGHT: The first passenger trains over the newly-built Canadian Pacific mainline north of Lake Superior were troop trains, carrying soldiers from the east to the scene of the Northwest Rebellion on the prairies.

BELOW: C.P.R 285, the first locomotive built by Canadian Pacific Railways.

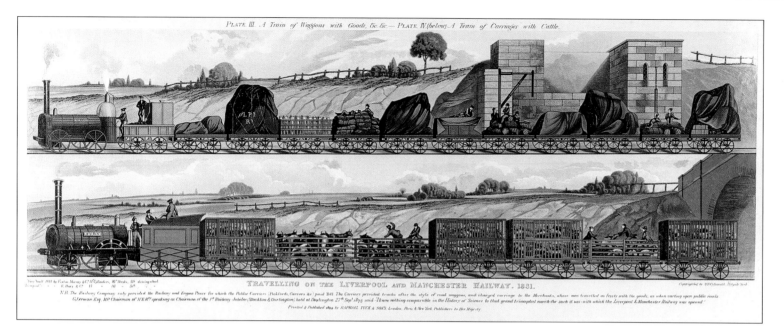

ABOVE: *Travelling on the Liverpool &*
Manchester Railway, 1831. Top: Goods
train drawn by Liverpool. *Bottom: Cattle*
train pulled by Fury.

BELOW: *Top: 1st-class carriages hauled*
by Jupiter. *Bottom: 2nd- and 3rd-class*
carriages drawn by North Star.

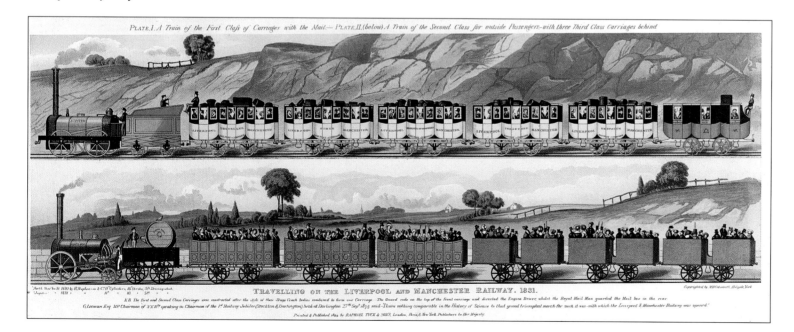

should perhaps be replaced by an appreciation that each is essential to the other. The spread of short-distance rail services from stations located strategically in the central areas of a metropolis to serve as termini for services to and from outlying areas allowed the development of the metropolis as a commercial and administrative centre serviced by workers for whom working rather than living space had to be found. Workers were eventually able to commute on a daily basis to and from their places of work in the metropolis and their homes in the suburbs whose rapid growth turned them into conurbations of the metropolis with the core surrounded by a ring of self-contained towns linked to the metropolis by commuter rail services.

This situation first developed in the areas around major cities, typically London and New York, but the process then acquired an almost inevitable momentum of its own, and as the complexity of modern life gradually approached the point of choking other increasingly important cities with traffic and a high level of pollution, large parts of their growing populations opted to move to suburbs linked to the city proper by rail services. This tendency was first apparent in other European and North American cities, but the development of important centres of government, commerce and industry in other regions has seen the development of basically the same concept in countries as widely separated as Australia, Brazil, India and Japan, whose major cities have gradually become conurbations as their cores are surrounded

ABOVE LEFT: *In its eagerness to push towards Utah in its race with the westward-building Union Pacific, Central Pacific bridged many of the High Sierra chasms with timber trestles. When the railroad was completed, they came back and the Chinese labourers that built the railroad filled them in with solid earth and embankments.*

ABOVE: *The Union locomotive* Fred Leach *after escaping from the Confederates. The holes in the smokestack show where the shots struck while she was working on the Orange & Alexandria Railroad near Inion Mills. 1 August 1863.*

LEFT: *Replica Baltimore & Ohio Railroad* Atlantic *heads a train at the Fair of the Iron Horse, Seattle, 1927.*

by belts of suburbs and growing commuter networks still based largely on the train even though road transport has eroded its previously predominant position. In this instance it is worthy of note that the improvements in the creature comforts enjoyed by long-distance passengers were generally not mirrored in the trains built for the commuter; rather it was believed that the monopoly in this short-distance trade could be made most profitable by packing in the maximum numbers of passengers who, in realistic terms, had no other means of travelling between their places of work and their homes.

In overall terms, therefore, it can be seen that the commuter services not only provided an essential service for suburban areas, but also helped to create and fashion

OPPOSITE: A refurbished 4-4-0 representing Jupiter *at Promontory Point, Utah, from Cecil B. DeMille's movie* Union Pacific.

ABOVE: A still of the Golden Spike ceremony at Promontory Point, Utah, from Cecil B. DeMille's movie Union Pacific.

ABOVE RIGHT: Driving in the golden rivet (spike) in the ceremony connecting the Atlantic and Pacific by railroad. Promontary, Utah, 10 May 1869.

RIGHT: Union Pacific construction train, 1868.

ABOVE LEFT: *Ruins of the Confederate engine-house at Atlanta, Georgia showing the engines* Telegraph *and* O.A. Bull *in September 1864.*

ABOVE RIGHT: *A construction crew of the 1850s.*

LEFT: *A scene on the Union Pacific Railroad in 1868 showing a construction train from General Casement's outfit near the railhead at Bear River City. Such trains included flat cars for tools, a forge for blacksmithing, coaches for sleeping and other cars for cooking, eating and storage.*

OPPOSITE
ABOVE LEFT: *Construction of the Northern Pacific Railroad at Big Rock, one mile above Cabinet.*

ABOVE RIGHT: *An historic occasion when Great Northern officials drove the final spike into a roughly hewn cross tie to complete a continuous track from Minnesota's twin cities to Puget Sound, Cascade Mountains on 6 January 1893.*

BELOW: *Crew of the first train west of the Big Savage Tunnel near Deal, Maryland on the Western Maryland Railroad, 29 October 1911.*

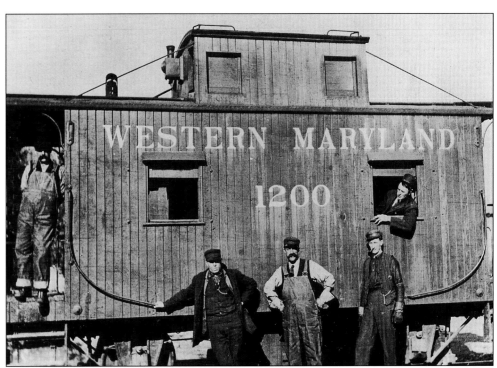

them as additional suburbs were generally built close to suburban commuter rail lines.

In the areas removed from the major conurbations, the railway and railroad companies operated slower branch services to cater for the needs of these smaller and less bustling towns. In concept, this type of service was different from that designed for the commuter, which had to make frequent stops at closely-spaced stations. Branch services, on the other hand, largely connected rural towns that were more widely separated, possessed smaller populations, and were in no real way wholly dependent on the train services. These branch services generally linked their mainline services to a town of modest size, but were generally created by local interests as a convenience rather than a total

necessity. As a result, the profit margins of such operations were small if not absent, and the speed of their services was low. The importance of such branch services should not be underestimated, however, for they were of considerable importance in allowing the relatively rapid transport of farm produce from the country to the metropolis in the period before the useful life of such produce could be economically extended by refrigeration.

Given the fact that it was in the U.K. that the railway began life as a commercial proposition, it was inevitable that it should be the British experience, at the practical as well as the theoretical level, that was widely responsible for stimulating the creation of fledgling railways and railroads in many other parts of the world. This naturally

included the export of the hardware required for these developments, for the U.K. was the world's leading manufacturing and exporting nation of the period. British companies did export relatively simple items such as rails, but these were soon manufactured in most of the countries in which they were used, so of greater long-term importance was the export of key features of the rolling stock (axles, wheels etc.), as well as complete steam locomotives, of which the first 'best seller' was the Stephenson 'Patentee', a 2-2-2 type that was extensively used on pioneering rail networks all over the world. This technical lead and export skill combined with the

ABOVE LEFT: On 31 December 1886 the city council of Fort Madison, Iowa passed an ordinance granting the Chicago, Santa Fe and California Railroad the right to construct in Iowa. On 1 January 1887, construction work began on the Fort Madison embankment.

ABOVE: Inspection Locomotive No. 1370, built at Beardstown in 1886. It was later renumbered twice, and was retired in June, 1924.

LEFT: The first Northern Pacific passenger train into Minnewaukon. The engine was called Dakota, *the fireman was William Buckley and the engineer George Kingsley.*

ABOVE: *An 1882 poster by Swaim & Lewis advertising the Illinois Central Railroad.*

LEFT TOP: *An early 4-6-0 locomotive on the Santa Fe Railway at Burlingame.*

CENTRE: *A Wendell Bollman truss bridge crossing the Monorgahela River near Fairmont, West Virginia. Originally a single track, it was later doubled and carried traffic between 1852 and the 1930s.*

BOTTOM: *Baltimore & Ohio Railroad bridge over the Ohio river between Benwood, West Virginia and Bellaire, Ohio, built in 1871.*

nature of the U.K. in the Victorian age as the world's most significant financial and colonial power, made it inevitable that British railway expertise would extend far and wide.

Railway networks were of signal importance to the British as they extended and consolidated their empire in the second half of the 19th century, and the spread of rail transport was instrumental in helping them to open up large areas of hitherto undeveloped territory. To this extent, therefore, burgeoning rail networks in the empire had very considerable economic and social impact. However, most of them were also of strategic importance, and many

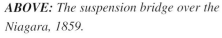

ABOVE: *The suspension bridge over the Niagara, 1859.*

ABOVE RIGHT: *Construction of the* chemin de fer *in Guinea, Africa.*

RIGHT: *The locomotive* Minnetonka *of the Northern Pacific Railroad, purchased in 1870 for use in construction work in northern Minnesota.*

OPPOSITE: *A train crosses Stockport Viaduct on the London & North Western Railway. Note pollution of river banks, smoking chimneys, and complete domination of the scene by the railway viaduct. (Coloured lithograph circa 1845.)*

came complete with a large measure of military input in their location and design so that troops and their equipment could be moved rapidly and surely from main base areas to potential trouble spots. This latter was useful in terms of cost effectiveness, for it allowed the British to garrison their colonial possessions with far fewer troops than would otherwise have been the case: instead of maintaining a small but potentially vulnerable and highly costly garrison in every small region, the British were able to use the strategic mobility provided by the railways to move troops as and when needed.

Some of the earliest colonial railways

appeared in India, a large, highly populated and very rich country with only a small industrial base. The first railway in India was inaugurated between Bombay and Thana as early as 1853, but in the short term the size of the country and its distance from the U.K. meant that development of a comprehensive railway network was slow. However, as a result of the efforts of one of the country's most far-sighted and effective governors general, Lord Dalhousie, India then developed a very well planned network of railway services that grew steadily in overall size and concept. By 1870 there were lines, each more than 1,000 miles (1600km) long, linking major centres such as Delhi and Calcutta on the one hand and Bombay and Calcutta on the other, and a mere 10 years later the network totalled 9,000 miles (14500km). This length of track may seem, and indeed is small in a country the size of India, which at the time included

LEFT: The Hercules, *built by Garret & Eastwich of Philadelphia in 1837 for the Beaver Meadow Railroad. The locomotive weighed 15 tons, an exceptionally large engine for the period.*

BELOW LEFT: The 1856 Baltimore & Ohio 4-4-0 locomotive William Mason, *posed at the Fair of the Iron Horse, Baltimore. 1927.*

BELOW RIGHT: Chicago & North Western Railroad's The Pioneer *4-2-0.*

OPPOSITE
ABOVE LEFT: A train on the Takanawa Railroad, Japan, circa 1880.

ABOVE RIGHT:
The Express Train, *a print published by Currier & Ives, New York 1870.*

BELOW RIGHT: A Pullman carriage of 1876.

what are now Bangladesh and Pakistan. But the effect of the network was augmented by its careful planning and execution.

The most radical aspect of British railway planning in Africa may have been the 'Cape to Cairo' line planned and partially completed by Cecil Rhodes, as noted above, but it was far from being the only British development on the continent, where there was an enormous surge of railway construction in the period between 1880 and 1920. As in India, there was always an element of strategic thinking in the developments of these lines, which generally reached inland from the main ports to areas of major population and/or economic importance, and typical of the process was the line, more than 500 miles (800km) long, constructed between the Gold Coast (now Ghana) and the deep interior of the country to allow the

development of important exports such as manganese, cocoa and timber. The construction of the line, in a gauge of 3ft 6in (1.067m), was completed in the face of a host of obstacles (man-made such as tribal uprisings and natural hazards such as huge ravines and apparently numberless diseases) before the line could start useful work.

Another part of the British empire that secured a major advantage from the local construction of railways was Australia. Here the evolution of the system was fragmented, for it was developed largely for and around the very widely separated centres of population rather than as a means of linking these centres, and a number of different gauges were used, the most popular being a gauge of 3ft 6in (1.067m), but there were also tracks with gauges of 5ft 3in (1.60m) and 4ft 8½in (1.432m).

1876

THE STEADY MARCH OF PROGRESS CENTENNIAL YEAR—1876—opened a period of further progress. The car's length grew from 58 to 70 feet. Oil lamps superseded candles. Air brakes appeared, making for greater speed and safety. A hot water heating system replaced stoves and furnaces. Six-wheel trucks were definitely adopted and overhead tanks with gravity supply system afforded water. Interior finish was in walnut, with carving, inlaying and lacquer work characteristic of the period.

OPPOSITE: Three lines converged in western South Dakota in the 1880s. On top is a local mine railroad, in the centre the Fremont, Elkhorn & Missouri Valley (a Chicago and North Western subsidiary), while below is a predecessor of today's Burlington Northern.

RIGHT: Plush coach accommodation before the turn of the century.

FAR RIGHT: Interior of the Northern Pacific Railroad's North Coast Limited *in April 1900, the first train lit by electricity to cross the north-west.*

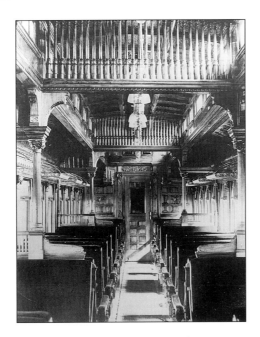

RIGHT: A Union Pacific 4-4-0 of 1870, with its smoke-arresting smokestack, cowcatcher and simple rugged construction that made this locomotive type so suitable for 'frontier' country.

ABOVE: North American Indians who have left their reservation and are attacking a train on the Southern Pacific Railroad, Arizona. The picture was taken from a weekly journal published in Paris in February 1906.

RIGHT: An advertisement for the Chicago & North Western Railroad's Short Line.

LEFT: Metropolitan Railway Electric Locomotive No.1, with a train of Ashkney coaches bound for Harrow, Middlesex, England in 1904.

BELOW: The first suburban train arriving at Park Ridge in 1874. The Chicago & North Western still carries close to 50,000 commuters daily on lines to the west, north and north-west.

Although much of the pioneering British experience in railway planning and construction was initially exported to the British Empire, it was also spread to other countries, both independent and the colonies of other European powers. It was the growth of this export trade that turned several middle-sized British companies into large operators, and typical of this process were the Vulcan Foundry of Newton-le-Willows in Lancashire, Beyer Peacock of Manchester, Hunslet of Leeds, and North British of Scotland. Thus the British railway influence in parts of the world outside Europe stretched far wider than its imperial context: the development of South American railways involved the activity of many British railway companies, who constructed lines all over the continent and included the privately British-owned Buenos Aires Great Southern Railway, which had over 5,000 miles (8000km) of track in Argentina, and the British-owned Buenos Aires Great Western Railway that had 1,000 miles (1600km) of track in Argentina. The two most important Chilean railway operators were the Antofagasta Railway and the Nitrate Railway Company, and both of these were British-owned. Inevitably, many of the steam locomotives and much of the rolling

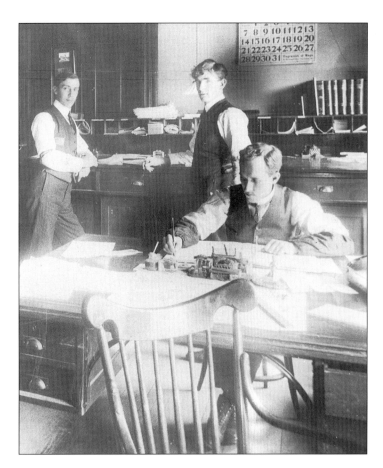

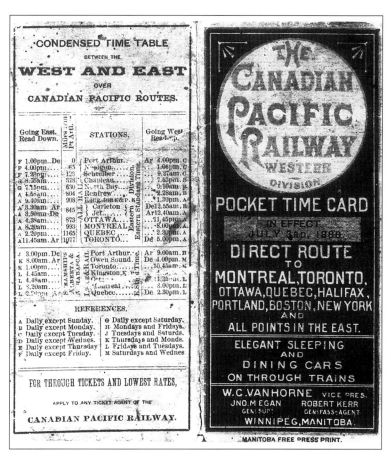

LEFT: *The North-West railway station, Vienna in a painting by Karl Karger, circa 1890.*

ABOVE: *A group of Toronto, Hamilton & Buffalo Railway employees in their office.*

ABOVE: *Front and back covers of a Canadian Pacific Railway (Western Division) pocket time card. This issue came into effect on 3 July 1886.*

LEFT: The Station, *a painting by Frith from 1862.*

RIGHT: *Harrisburg, Pennsylvania, the station in the 1860s just after the American Civil War. Shown here are trains operated by four railroads: Pennsylvania, Northern Central, Cumberland Valley and the Philadelphia & Reading. The first three are now included in the Pennsylvania Railroad system.*

BELOW RIGHT: *An old Grand Trunk railway station at St.Williams, Ontario, Canada.*

stock for these lines was manufactured by British companies.

As the 19th century progressed, however, the British share of the export market was eroded by the increasing success of rival companies, especially those of the U.S.A. This increasing level of export success resulted in part from the increasing size and skill of the American industrial machine, whose rapid growth had been kick-started in the north of the country by the requirements of the Civil War, but also in part by the technical success of American steam locomotives, which were becoming increasingly different from their British counterparts in features such as bar-frame rather than plate-frame construction, 'haystack' fireboxes and, perhaps most

importantly of all, great ruggedness and reliability. This last factor stemmed from the size of the American railroad network and in combination with the relative paucity of towns in which major repairs or even routine maintenance could be undertaken. Thus steam locomotives of American design and manufacture were seldom as attractive in external shape as their European counterparts, but on the other hand were very reliable, easy to maintain and powerful. This last was of singular importance in many parts of South America, for instance, where it was the norm for heavy trains to be operated over lines with frequent gradients of a severity seldom encountered in the U.K. and Europe.

OPPOSITE
ABOVE LEFT and RIGHT: Steam-coaches on the Pilatus rack railway in Switzerland. These vehicles were characteristic of the Pilatus, the passenger coach and locomotive being built in one to save weight. The driver and stoker rode in the cab at the valley end, while passengers and conductor travelled on the upper platforms.

BELOW: Japanese during the Russo-Japanese War, firing on a Russian Red Cross train on the Trans-Siberian Railway carrying wounded to Port Arthur. From a weekly newspaper published in Paris on 15 May 1904.

ABOVE LEFT: A passenger train pauses in front of the Toronto, Hamilton & Buffalo Railway station and offices.

ABOVE: La Gare du Midi, Brussels, 1902.

LEFT: Russian cavalry during the Russo-Japanese War on their way to the Manchurian Front, crossing a river on a raft after disembarking from the Trans-Siberian Railway. (Illustration from a weekly paper published in Paris in 1904.)

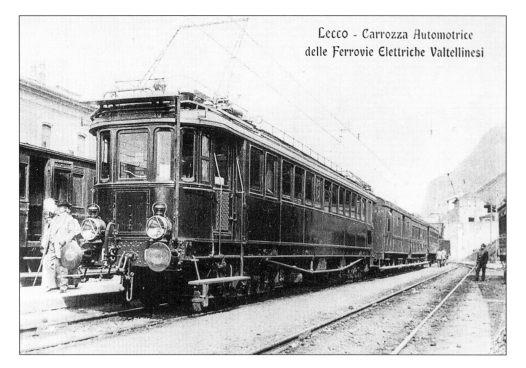

Lecco - Carrozza Automotrice delle Ferrovie Elettriche Valtellinesi

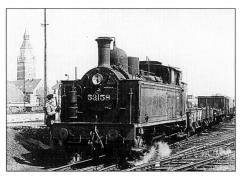

CLOCKWISE FROM TOP LEFT: *Type E1 electric unit on the Società Adriatica's Valtellinesi line at Lecco, waiting to leave for Colico, 1904.*

Union troops at City Point, Virginia await train transport to the front in 1864.

Belgian State Railway's 2-4-0 Vienna Express *leaving Ostend.*

Construction of the Pont de la Samakousse on the chemin de fer, Guinea, Africa 1902.

A Belgian saddle-tank moves freight in the late 1940s.

A Belgian railway steam train.

OPPOSITE

ABOVE: *View of Bombay Churchgate Station built in 1893, in a photograph taken in the 1920s.*

BELOW LEFT: *U.S. Military Railroad's engine* General Haupt, *named after General Hermann Haupt, Chief of Construction and Transportation for the Union armies. The locomotive was built in 1863.*

BELOW RIGHT: *Construction of the Pont de la Douona on the* chemin de fer, *Guinea, Africa.*

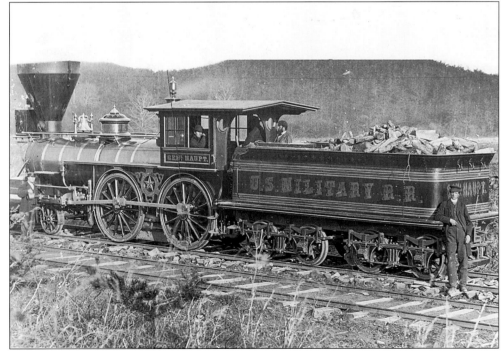

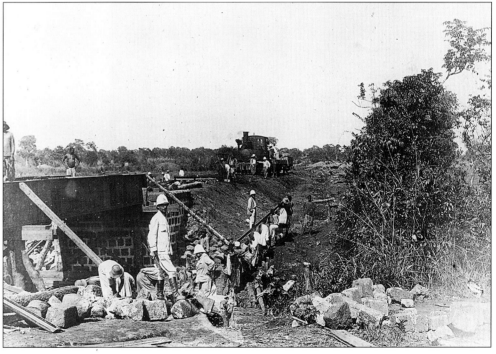

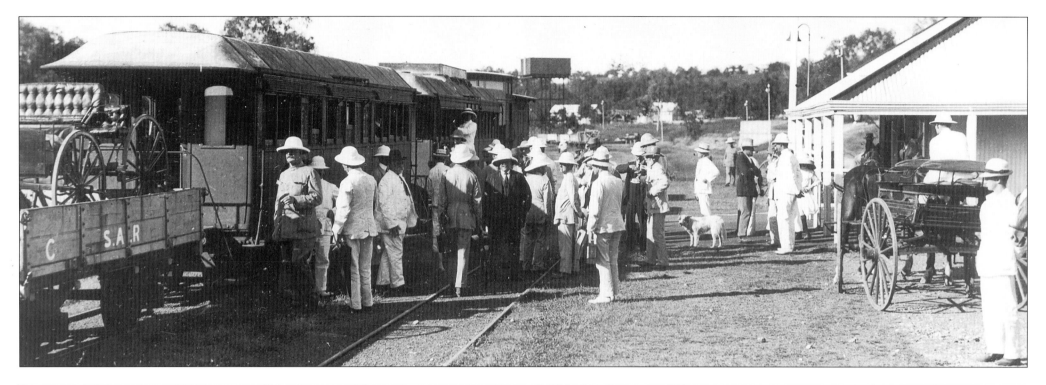

American steam locomotives for the export market differed enormously in size, from small tank locomotives to large articulated ones to cater for the full range of operating requirements, and the most common wheel arrangements were the 2-6-0, 2-8-0, 2-8-2 and 2-10-2 layouts. The first U.S. exports of steam locomotives were made, naturally enough, to neighbouring countries (Canada and Mexico), but their geographical extent later spread to South America, and then to markets that had hitherto been dominated by the British: these last included Australia, India, New Zealand and South Africa. American companies also managed to secure sales of their steam locomotives to Russia.

OPPOSITE
ABOVE: *Darwin railway station, Australia, circa 1900.*

BELOW: *Tarcoon railway station, New South Wales, circa 1900.*

RIGHT: *The 125th anniversary Victorian Government Railways 4-6-0.*

Picture Acknowledgements

Mechanical, Archive & Research Services, London, England: pages 16 left, 20 top right, 22 bottom, 23 both, 24 below, 43 below, 48 below right

Military Archive & Research Services, Lincolnshire, England: pages 4, 10 left, 14 top right, 20 bottom left, 25 top right, 27 below right, 28, 33, 34 below left and right, 39 top right, 40, 42 top left and right, 47 top left, 47 top right, 49 below, 51 top left, 59 top right, 60 top right (above and below), 60 below right, below left (above and below), 61 below left, 61 below right

*Association of American Railroads, U.S.A.: pages 19 below, 26 below, 48 top, 51 top right, 57 top

*B.C. Provincial Archives: pages 31 right, 36

*Baltimore & Ohio Railroad: pages 14 below left, 18 right, 21 both, 22 top left, 25 below, 32 top left, 34 top, 39 below, 45 left centre and below, 48 below left

*Burlington Northern Railroad: page 50

*Canadian National: pages 30, 57 below

*Canadian Pacific Corporate Archives: pages 27 left, 31 right, 32 top right, 35 top, 37 both, 55 top left and right, spanning top of pages 58–59

*Chicago & North Western Railroad: page 53 below

*Chicago, Burlington & Quincy Railroad: pages 35 below right, 44 top right

*Delaware & Hudson Railroad: page 18 left

* © Denver Public Library, Western History Department: page 19 below

*Great Northern Railroad: page 43 top right

*Gulf Oil Company: page 26 top

*Holloway College: page 56

*Indian National Railways, Delhi: page 61 above

*Italian State Railways: pages 29 top left and bottom left and right, 60 top left

*Library of Congress: pages 25 top left, 45 top right

*London Transport: page 53 above

*Milwaukee Road: page 52 right

*National Gallery of Art, Washington, D.C.: title pages

*National Library of Australia: page 62 both

*National Railway Museum, York, England: page 20 top left

*Nelson Gallery, Atkins Museum: page 24 top

*Northern Pacific Railroad: pages 43 top left, 44 below, 47 below

*Österreichische Galerie: page 54

*Santa Fe Railway: pages 32 below, 44 top left, 45 left top

*Science Museum, London: page 12

*Southern Pacific Transportation Co.: page 39 top left

*Swiss National Tourist Office, Zürich: page 27 top right

*Union Pacific Railroad: pages 35 bottom left, 41 top left, 42 below, 51 below

*Victorian Railways: page 63

*York County Historical Society: page 22 top right

Pilatus Railway, Lucerne: prints from JG Moore Collection, London: page 58 top left and centre

Ann Ronan at Image Select, London: pages 5, 6, 7 all, 8 below left and top right, 9, 10 right, 11 all, 13 all, 14 top left and bottom right, 16 centre and right, 17, 20 bottom right, 29 top right, 38 both, 41 top right and below, 46, 49 top left and right, 52 left, 58 below, 59 below

* Prints through **Military Archive & Research Services, Lincolnshire, England**